The Elections of 2012 Outcomes and Analysis

CQ Press, an imprint of SAGE, is the leading publisher of books, periodicals, and electronic products on American government and international affairs. CQ Press consistently ranks among the top commercial publishers in terms of quality, as evidenced by the numerous awards its products have won over the years. CQ Press owes its existence to Nelson Poynter, former publisher of the *St. Petersburg Times*, and his wife Henrietta, with whom he founded Congressional Quarterly in 1945. Poynter established CQ with the mission of promoting democracy through education and in 1975 founded the Modern Media Institute, renamed The Poynter Institute for Media Studies after his death. The Poynter Institute (*www.poynter.org*) is a nonprofit organization dedicated to training journalists and media leaders.

In 2008, CQ Press was acquired by SAGE, a leading international publisher of journals, books, and electronic media for academic, educational, and professional markets. Since 1965, SAGE has helped inform and educate a global community of scholars, practitioners, researchers, and students spanning a wide range of subject areas, including business, humanities, social sciences, and science, technology, and medicine. A privately owned corporation, SAGE has offices in Los Angeles, London, New Delhi, and Singapore, in addition to the Washington DC office of CQ Press.

The Elections of 2012 Outcomes and Analysis

Chuck McCutcheon

Los Angeles | London | New Delhi
Singapore | Washington DC

Los Angeles | London | New Delhi
Singapore | Washington DC

FOR INFORMATION:

CQ Press
An Imprint of SAGE Publications, Inc.
2455 Teller Road
Thousand Oaks, California 91320
E-mail: order@sagepub.com

SAGE Publications Ltd.
1 Oliver's Yard
55 City Road
London EC1Y 1SP
United Kingdom

SAGE Publications India Pvt. Ltd.
B 1/I 1 Mohan Cooperative Industrial Area
Mathura Road, New Delhi 110 044
India

SAGE Publications Asia-Pacific Pte. Ltd.
3 Church Street
#10-04 Samsung Hub
Singapore 049483

Acquisitions Editor: Charisse Kiino
Editorial Assistant: Nancy Loh
Production Editor: Laura Barrett
Copy Editor: Amy Marks
Typesetter: C&M Digitals (P) Ltd.
Proofreader: Annie Lubinsky
Cover Designer: Karine Hovsepian
Marketing Manager: Jonathan Mason
Permissions Editor: Karen Ehrmann

Printed in the United States of America

A catalog record of this book is available from the Library of Congress.

ISBN 978-1-4522-2787-0

This book is printed on acid-free paper.

SFI label applies to text stock

12 13 14 15 16 10 9 8 7 6 5 4 3 2 1

Contents

OUTLINE:

AP Photo/Jerome Delay.

A jubilant President Barack Obama celebrates with his wife, Michelle, and Vice President Joe Biden on Election Night in Chicago. Obama took 332 electoral votes and 50.5 percent of the popular vote to 206 electoral votes and 47.9 percent of the popular vote for Mitt Romney.

The 2012 Elections Broke the Rules of Politics

The 2012 elections were historic for defying the normal rules of politics. Those rules dictated that an incumbent president presiding over a lackluster economy, with an unemployment rate stuck around 8 percent, stood no chance of being reelected. The rules also stipulated that a candidate who received six out of every ten votes from white Americans, the single largest voting demographic, and substantial financial backing from outside interests, was practically guaranteed to win. In addition, they said that a Congress with record-low levels of popularity was destined to see big shifts in party control.

Yet the rules were upended. President Barack Obama easily won a second term, winning both the popular vote and the Electoral College despite Americans' dissatisfaction with the economy's performance. Overwhelming support from minorities—Obama won almost three-quarters of the votes of both Hispanics and Asians, and more than 90 percent of the African American vote—more than offset Republican challenger Mitt Romney's robust performance among white voters and the hundreds of millions of dollars he received from "super PACs" that financed television ads attacking the president and other Democrats.

Romney had sought to make the election a referendum on Obama's handling of the economy, which he and his running mate, Rep. Paul Ryan of Wisconsin, said was recovering too sluggishly because of Obama's inability to understand how to manage it. But Obama portrayed Romney as someone with an inability to understand average Americans. He cast the race as an opportunity to expand on the achievements of his first term—enacting health care reform, reinvigorating the domestic automobile industry, winding down the wars in Iraq and Afghanistan—while giving people of all incomes as much chance as the wealthy to succeed.

> "I believe we can build on the progress we've made and continue to fight for new jobs and new opportunity and new security for the middle class," the president told cheering supporters in Chicago on Election Night. "I believe we can keep the promise of our founders, the idea that if you're willing to work hard, it doesn't matter who you are or where you come from or what you look like . . . you can make it here in America if you're willing to try."[1]

In an equally surprising development, Democrats were able to retain their majority status in the Senate. Republicans lost their opportunity to pick up several Democratic-held seats by nominating conservative candidates who were popular with their like-minded base but who could not sway more independent-minded voters—and who, in two cases, made highly controversial remarks on abortion and rape that spelled their doom at the polls.

The Democrats' good fortune extended to the statehouses. Republicans poured tens of millions of dollars into an effort to gain control of more governors' offices across the country, but managed only to wrest North Carolina from Democrats. Even states that voted heavily Republican in the presidential race, such as Montana, Missouri, and West Virginia, ended up electing Democratic governors. So did states that fielded seriously competitive GOP candidates, such as Washington and New Hampshire.

The lone bright spot for Republicans was their ability to keep their majority in the House of Representatives, even as Democrats picked up a handful of new seats there. The GOP's edge was attributed to redistricting after the 2010 census, in which Republican-led state legislatures redrew the geographic contours of congressional areas to make their candidates more electable.

But the Republicans' dismal performance both in the White House and in Senate contests provoked immediate calls for soul-searching among the GOP's leading adherents. They said their immediate challenge was to figure out how the Republican Party could remain viable in a country that was growing more culturally diverse and less attuned to its message—often aggressively broadcast—of limited government and hostility to compromise.

"We are in a position now where we have to—through differences in policy, differences in tone and differences in candidates—reach out in a way we've never reached out before," said Whit Ayres, a veteran Republican pollster. "Or we will not be successful as a national party."[2] Former Republican senator Mel Martinez of

Florida agreed that, in particular, the party needed to appeal to more Latinos: "This is not a choice. It's either extinction or survival."[3]

Beyond the Republican Party's quest to redefine itself, the election results indicated that Obama would gain leverage in the protracted battles he had fought against Republicans during his first term over spending and deficits—battles that had led to substantial Republican gains in the 2010 midterm elections. The results also yielded agreement that the politically elusive task of reforming the immigration system—an issue that had cost Romney politically among Hispanics—would become a high priority for both parties in 2013.

Demographics of the Election

Romney's success at winning his 2002 race for governor of Massachusetts provided the basis for the argument that he would be better suited than most Republicans to compete in other states that typically lean Democratic. His successful tenure as cofounder and CEO (chief executive officer) of Bain Capital, a Boston-based private equity firm best known for its corporate takeover and reorganization efforts, underscored his contention that the nation needed a president with a serious business background to fix the troubled economy and gave him substantial wealth—his estimated worth is about $250 million. He also is remembered for stepping in to head

AP Photo/*The Virginian-Pilot*, Amanda Lucier.

William Wright, left, and India Johnson, right, wait on line to vote in Norfolk, Virginia. African Americans accounted for 21 percent of those who voted in the state, with 94 percent of those backing the president.

FIGURE 1
2012 Election Results

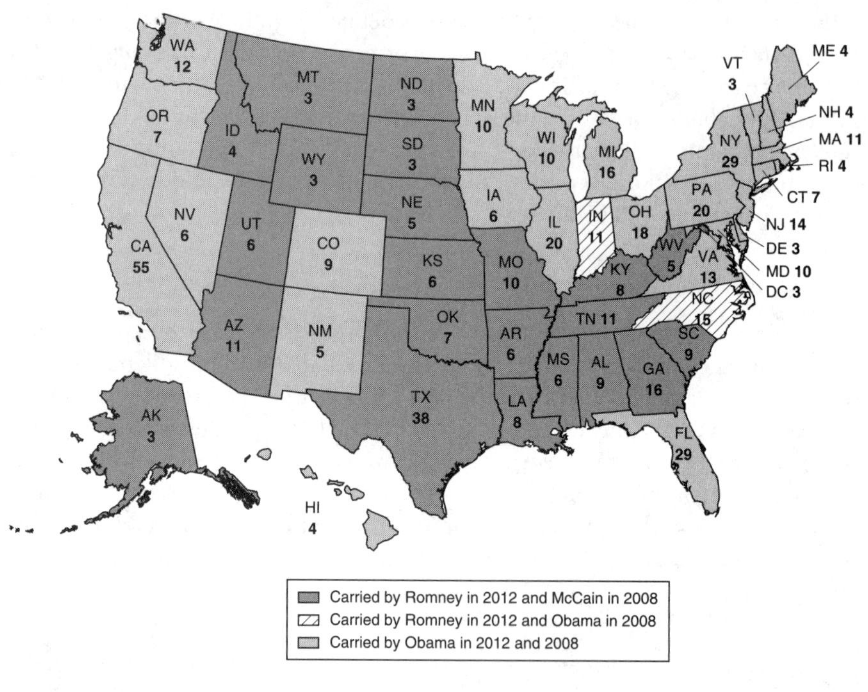

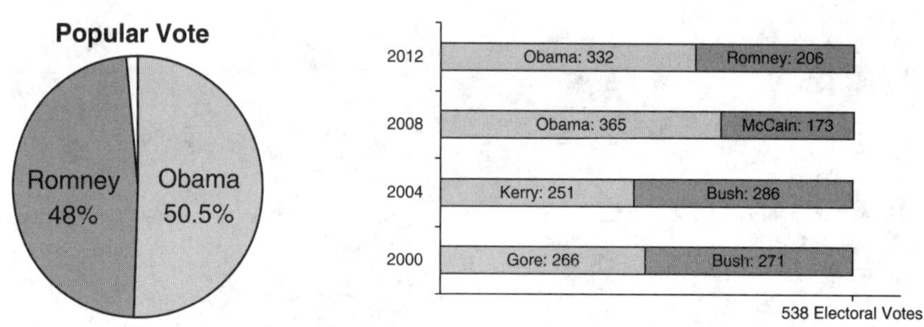

Source: "Obama's Path to Victory," *CQ Weekly*, Election 2012 Special Report, November 12, 2012, p. 2207.

and successfully stage the Winter Olympic Games held in Salt Lake City, Utah, in early 2002 after the event was put at risk by financial scandals.

But with the exception of North Carolina, which Obama had narrowly won in 2008, Romney was unable to carry any of the most competitive "battleground" states. Obama prevailed despite his rival's sustained efforts in states such as Ohio, Florida,

Virginia, Wisconsin, New Hampshire, and Colorado. The president also easily won the traditional Democratic strongholds of California and New York and other populous states such as Michigan, the state where Romney was born and his father served as governor, as well as Massachusetts and Pennsylvania. He won a total of 647 electoral votes in 2008 and 2012—fewer than Bill Clinton's 749 in 1992 and 1996, but much more than George W. Bush's 557 in 2000 and 2004.

Obama relied on a superior get-out-the-vote operation carried over from 2008, in which potential supporters were catalogued and tracked to determine their Election Day decisions. But Romney's campaign also made several miscalculations about turnout:

- It did not figure that Obama would receive even greater African American or Hispanic support than he had previously won. Blacks in Ohio, Virginia, North Carolina, and Florida all backed the president in greater numbers than they did in 2008. Similarly, Obama won 73 percent of the Asian American vote and 71 percent of the Hispanic vote; in Florida, the share of Hispanic voters rose from 14 percent in 2008 to 17 percent. Put another way, 72 percent of the electorate was white, the lowest proportion ever and a sizeable drop from 20 years earlier, when it stood at 87 percent. Obama voters showed their enthusiasm in early voting as well as on Election Day; many stood in lines for hours in areas of South Florida, and polling places in some parts of Virginia were held open for hours after the scheduled 7 p.m. closing to accommodate waiting voters.

- It underestimated Romney's support among independent voters, having seen pre-election polls that showed Romney running strongly among that demographic. But exit polls showed that many of the independents were former Republicans who had switched their affiliation. The two candidates ended up splitting the independent vote—but Obama won more of that vote in key states such as Iowa and New Hampshire.

- It assumed that most of the last-minute undecided voters would side with Romney. The common perception is that challengers of incumbents generally win those voters, since people are familiar with the incumbent and would have decided already if they were backing him. But exit polls showed Obama prevailed among voters who made up their minds in the few days before the election and on Election Day.

Obama's success, however, went beyond capturing minority and independent voters. His triumphs in Ohio, Iowa, and Wisconsin were rooted in a message of economic populism that resonated with working-class whites, the bedrock of the Democratic Party's coalition in the twentieth century. In Ohio, the Obama administration's successful bailout for General Motors Corp. and Chrysler Corp.—which Romney had criticized—was seen as the decisive factor. The auto sector was responsible for some 800,000 jobs in eighty of the state's eighty-eight counties.

The 2012 election also saw a surge in the share of unmarried voters, who made up 41 percent of the electorate, up from 34 percent in 2008. Obama won this group decisively, with 62 percent of the vote. Single women, in particular, favored the president by 38 percentage points over Romney. Some said in exit polls that what they saw as conservatives' overreach on social issues such as abortion negatively impacted their view of Romney.

TABLE 1
Who Voted and How?

	Percentage who voted for Obama	Percentage who voted for Romney
Gender		
Male (47%)	45%	52%
Female (53%)	55%	44%
Age		
18–29 (19%)	60%	37%
30–44 (27%)	52%	45%
45–65 (38%)	47%	51%
65 or over (16%)	44%	56%
Married		
Yes	42%	56%
No	62%	35%
Race/Ethnicity		
White (72%)	39%	59%
Black (13%)	93%	6%
Hispanic/Latino (10%)	71%	27%
Asian (3%)	73%	26%
Other (2%)	58%	38%
Education		
No high school diploma (3%)	64%	35%
High school graduate (21%)	51%	48%
Some college/assoc. degree (29%)	49%	48%
College graduate (29%)	47%	51%
Postgraduate study (18%)	55%	42%
Income		
Under $30,000 (20%)	63%	35%
$30,000–$49,999 (21%)	57%	42%
$50,000–$99,999 (31%)	46%	52%
$100,000–$199,999 (21%)	44%	54%
$200,000–$249,000 (3%)	47%	52%
Over $250,000 (4%)	42%	55%
Geography		
City over 50,000 (32%)	62%	36%
Suburbs (47%)	48%	50%
Small city and rural (21%)	39%	59%

Source: ABC News 2012 Exit Polls, abcnews.go.com/politics/elections/National?ep=pre_na.

And though Obama did not reach the two-thirds level of support from younger votes that he won in 2008, that demographic still gave him 60 percent of their vote. Despite many predictions that disaffected younger voters would stay home, they matched their participation rate from 2008, with about half of eligible voters under age 30 casting ballots. More important for the president, they increased their share of the electorate over four years, from 18 percent to 19 percent—and in so doing surpassed the proportion of voters (17 percent) over age 65 who predominantly backed Romney.

Republican Super PAC Spending Doesn't Help

The 2012 election was the most expensive in history. The Center for Responsive Politics, a leading campaign finance watchdog group, estimated its overall cost at $6 billion. The presidential race alone accounted for $2.6 billion, which represented a decrease from 2008, when nearly $2.8 billion was directed at the presidential race. House and Senate races grew more expensive to make up the difference.

The election was the first presidential contest to be held following the Supreme Court's landmark *Citizens United v. Federal Election Commission* decision in 2010. That highly controversial ruling held that corporate funding of independent political broadcasts in candidate elections could not be limited because of the First Amendment, paving the way for corporations and other wealthy interests to make unlimited contributions on a candidate's behalf.

Many Democrats, including Obama, condemned the decision because they said it undermined the influence of average Americans who make small contributions to

John Branch.

support their preferred candidates. The ruling was seen as a key factor in helping Republicans recapture control of the House in 2010, and paved the way for the $970 million spent in 2012 by super PACs and other independent outside groups such as nonprofit organizations.

Restore Our Future, the super PAC supporting Romney's presidential campaign, spent an estimated $125 million. Priorities USA Action, the super PAC backing Obama, spent less than half as much. The largest of the groups was American Crossroads and its nonprofit "social welfare" counterpart, Crossroads GPS, organizations founded by prominent GOP strategist Karl Rove. Together those groups reported spending more than $158 million on independent expenditures and election-related communications on behalf of Romney and other Republicans.

In the days following Romney's defeat, Rove came under punishing criticism from an assortment of conservatives for failing to achieve the desired results despite having raised and spent so much. Richard Viguerie, a leading conservative activist, wrote that "in any logical universe," wrongheaded strategists such as Rove "would never be hired to run or consult on a national campaign again—and no one would give a dime to their ineffective super PACs."[4]

Analysts said that conservative super PACs tended to prize ideological purity among favored candidates, in keeping with their donors' wishes. But in many cases, those candidates ended up having trouble reaching independent voters partly because they were seemingly immune to moderating their views—a tough sell in a country in which voters had grown weary of polarization.

FIGURE 2
Cost of U.S. Elections, 1998–2012

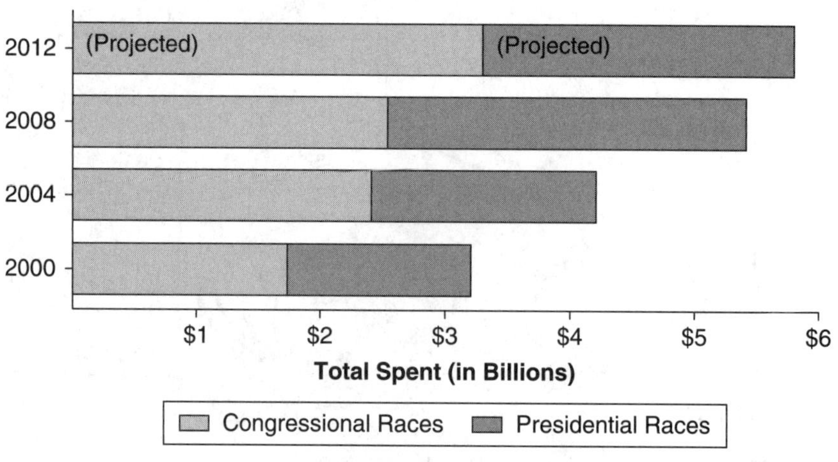

Source: Center for Responsive Politics, "The Money Behind the Elections," www.opensecrets.org, accessed November 14, 2012.

How the Presidential Race Unfolded

Romney Secures the Republican Nomination

Romney officially became the Republican presidential nominee on May 30 after winning Texas's presidential primary, providing him with the 1,144 delegates he needed to capture the nomination. The milestone came after his closest and fiercest rival, former senator Rick Santorum, suddenly decided on April 10 to quit the GOP race. Santorum's chances of capturing the GOP nomination had shrunk to nothing, and he faced the unpalatable prospect of losing to Romney in his home state of Pennsylvania.

"Our party has come together, with the goal of putting the failures of the last three and a half years behind us," Romney said when the Texas returns certified his status.[5]

The coming-together did not happen easily. Romney had been considered the Republican front-runner from the earliest days of the race, owing to his experience from running in 2008, his well-funded campaign organization, and his solid support among most of the national party establishment. Nevertheless, he had to endure a far more protracted primary process than he would have liked. Several of his rivals took turns briefly surging in the polls: Texas governor Rick Perry, former Godfather's Pizza executive Herman Cain and—most prominently—Santorum and former House Speaker Newt Gingrich.

Each of the would-be front-runners had political weaknesses that eventually revealed themselves during the primary season. In Perry's case, it was a thin grasp of policy that became apparent during a debate, when he could not remember the names of some Cabinet agencies that he wanted to abolish. For Cain, it was a lack of prior experience in government and a reliance on a single idea—simplifying taxes—as well as allegations of an extramarital affair.

Gingrich was hamstrung by his undisciplined campaign, which featured him articulating grandiose ideas such as colonizing the Moon. Santorum's ardent socially conservative views were seen as off-putting to moderate voters who were more interested in the economy. As some analysts pointed out, Romney didn't have to win as much as he had to wait for the others to lose.

Romney's chief problem in securing a critical mass of support in Republican primaries and caucuses was an enduring suspicion among many staunchly conservative voters that he did not stand as far to the right as he had positioned himself. His first political venture was a 1994 challenge to Massachusetts senator Edward M. Kennedy, and Romney in that campaign professed to be a supporter of abortion and gay rights, positions he said he altered in intervening years as he learned more about the issues. When he ran for governor in 2002, he cast himself as a conservative who would be able to negotiate with the Democrats who thoroughly dominated the Massachusetts legislature.

On the 2012 campaign trail, Romney went even further, describing himself as "severely conservative." Once a supporter of human-induced climate change, he later professed not to know what was responsible for accelerating levels of carbon dioxide and other greenhouse gases blamed for global warming. As governor, he had stood in front of a controversial coal-burning facility and declared, "This plant kills people." But in campaigning in coal-mining regions, he repeatedly accused Obama of engaging in a "war on coal."

To deal with illegal immigration, he called for those who had come to the United States illegally to "self-deport" and opposed the DREAM Act, a proposal backed by Gingrich and some other Republicans that had stalled in Congress. It aimed to provide a path to citizenship for children of undocumented immigrants who attend college or serve in the military. During a September 2011 debate, Romney accused Perry of creating a "magnet" for illegal immigrants by allowing Texas children to attend college with in-state tuition support through a state version of the measure; Perry responded that his rival lacked "a heart." Commentator Michael Gerson, a former George W. Bush speechwriter, later called the exchange "the lowest moment of the Romney campaign."[6]

Perhaps the biggest obstacle Romney faced in appealing to the Republican base was the fact that the landmark achievement of his four-year tenure as governor was shaping and signing into law a sweeping overhaul of the Massachusetts health

Republican presidential candidates Ron Paul, Rick Santorum, Mitt Romney, and Newt Gingrich take the stage at a debate in Mesa, Arizona. None of Romney's rivals established themselves as a credible threat to the former Massachusetts governor, who outraised all of them.

insurance system. The plan included an individual mandate, meaning that most of the state's citizens would be required to purchase health care coverage, either independently or through employer-provided insurance plans, with lower-income residents provided with means-tested government assistance to procure insurance. As a 2012 presidential candidate, Romney denied allusions by many Democrats, Republican opponents, and a number of independent analysts that his state law was a model for Obama's health insurance overhaul.

These provisions prompted Romney's Republican rivals for the nomination to brand the Massachusetts program as "Romneycare" and portray it as the model for the controversial federal legislation that they called "Obamacare." Democrats, seeking to make the campaign more difficult for Romney, concurred with that view and also accused Romney of hypocrisy for pledging to repeal and replace the health care measure that Obama had signed into law. But Romney denied that either was the case, stating that the program he had instituted in Massachusetts was shaped to the particular needs of that state's population and could not and should not be used as the baseline for a one-size-fits-all national program.

Many who had saluted Romney's achievements on health care and other issues as governor found his move to the political right unpalatable. New York City mayor Michael Bloomberg, an influential moderate, cited Romney's reversal on these positions—particularly climate change—as a reason to back Obama, a president with whom he had had many well-publicized differences. "In the past [Romney] has taken sensible positions . . . but he has reversed course on all of them," Bloomberg said in an editorial. "If the 1994 or 2003 version of Mitt Romney were running for president, I may well have voted for him."[7]

Romney's Chief Weapon—The Economy

From the outset, Romney made it clear that he would frame the general election around a single question—whether to continue or replace Obama because of what he termed the president's gross fiscal mismanagement. His 160-page economic plan led off with the assertion that Washington had weakened the United States' long-term growth prospects through its efforts to create jobs in the aftermath of the recession that Obama had inherited from President George W. Bush.

His view, developed in his years with Bain Capital, was that smaller government enables the private sector to create more productivity, more profits, and more jobs, with high levels of government spending discouraging private investment. Government regulation, he argued, only served to inhibit growth, while Obama's approach of pushing through economic stimulus bills merely masked structural economic problems.

Romney promised to send Congress a jobs package that would address several of his goals: It would reduce the top corporate income tax rate from 35 percent to 25 percent, slash $20 billion annually in domestic spending, expand domestic oil and gas drilling, and consolidate federal job-training programs. In addition to making permanent the tax cuts enacted under Bush, he proposed an across-the-board 20 percent tax cut for individuals. He also vowed to crack down on China for manipulating its currency and for remaining indifferent to intellectual property rights. He promised to cut nondefense discretionary spending by 5 percent and to cap federal spending at 20 percent of the country's gross domestic product by 2016, well below historic averages.

On the campaign trail, however, Romney devoted much of his time to fiercely criticizing Obama without articulating the specifics of those policies. For example, in a September appearance on NBC's *Meet the Press*, he sidestepped questions about what tax loopholes he would close to pay for his proposed tax cuts, saying only that he would seek to ease the burden on middle-income families. He said such an approach was consistent with his philosophy of governing, but the paucity of details dismayed even some conservative supporters. Publications such as the *Weekly Standard* called on him to spell out what he would do, and former Senate majority leader Trent Lott echoed that the candidate "needs to say clearly, 'You elect me, this is what you're going to get.'"[8]

The Obama campaign seized on that lack of clarity and used it to club its opponent, often telling voters that they would suffer the unexplained consequences of Romney's actions. As Vice President Joe Biden told an audience while campaigning in Milford, Ohio: "When you give these kinds of tax breaks out to the very, very wealthy, the money's got to come from somewhere. And guess who? You!"[9]

Building a Case against Romney

Obama's campaign also used another aspect of Romney's campaign against him—his reluctance to focus on his life story. A product of the corporate world rather than a natural politician, Romney disdained self-promotion, leaving it to his wife Ann to talk about his being a devoted father to their five sons. Until the end of the campaign, he rarely offered personal anecdotes in his speeches.

He also seldom discussed his Mormon faith, a religion that some religious conservatives regarded with skepticism. In particular, many evangelical Christians, who make up a substantial portion of the Republican electorate, have a history of hostility toward Mormonism because its doctrine includes its own interpretation of the Holy Scriptures. His attempts at connecting with average Americans occasionally came off as forced and, to many, elitist—he tried to show his affinity with Detroit's auto industry workers by mentioning that his wife drove "a couple of Cadillacs."

News articles often depicted Romney as coldly logical, making conclusions based on a rigorous examination of data rather than from some inner core conviction. The result was that Republican enthusiasm was driven more by a dislike of Obama than by admiration for Romney. One Pew Research Center poll in June showed 58 percent of those surveyed were motivated by their desire to oust Obama, compared to 38 percent who said they were motivated because of Romney.[10]

In sizing up a general-election race against Romney, Obama's advisers concluded they would have to run a much different campaign than the one of change and hope that had propelled their candidate into office four years earlier. More than anything, they felt they had to highlight the view among some voters that the wealthy Republican was too removed from their everyday lives to understand their concerns—something that his reticence did not permit him to refute easily. Consequently, the Obama campaign ran multiple television advertisements that highlighted how Bain Capital had shut down companies it had acquired, putting people out of work.

The Obama campaign and its Democratic surrogates also repeated charges that had been made during the Republican primary of Romney's refusal to shed light on his personal fortune—which included money in a Swiss bank account as well as an offshore account in the Cayman Islands. "When it comes down to his Swiss bank account, there is just no way to explain it," said Illinois Democratic senator Richard Durbin, a key Obama ally. "You either get a Swiss bank account to conceal what you're doing or you believe the Swiss franc is stronger than the American dollar."[11]

Durbin and other Democrats also incessantly called on Romney to release ten years of his income tax returns, something that his father, George, had done four decades earlier in his own presidential bid. During the primaries, Romney released his 2010 returns and an estimate for 2011; he subsequently released the full 2011 returns and a twenty-year listing of what tax rates he had paid, but not the actual returns. His campaign felt that any more material would only prove a distraction from its message.

As the Obama campaign hammered away at those issues, Romney often accused his rivals of misrepresenting his views. But Democrats responded that Romney was even guiltier of stretching the truth. One of the most common lines in the Republican's stump speech was his insistence that Obama had begun his presidency with an "apology tour" of other nations to offer regrets for past American actions. Romney titled his 2010 book *No Apology: The Case for American Greatness.* Although the new president had criticized what he called past U.S. mistakes, such as torturing suspected terrorists, he was widely considered not to have apologized. The fact-checking website PolitiFact gave the claim "Pants on Fire," its lowest rating for accuracy.[12]

Democrats were unapologetic in attacking their rival's character. They saw their approach as an implementation of the hard lesson learned in 2004, when their candidate—Massachusetts senator John Kerry—was perceived as not being willing to mix it up with Republicans and, as a result, did not recover from the infamous "Swift Boat" attacks in which fellow veterans questioned the details of his service in Vietnam. As Obama senior campaign adviser David Axelrod later said of Romney: "They didn't give people anything to grab on to, and they allowed us to define him before he could define himself."[13]

Picking Paul Ryan: A Race-Changing Moment

Well before Romney had wrapped up the Republican nomination, the guessing game about his running mate was in full swing. The conventional wisdom held that he would seek to avoid 2008 nominee John McCain's fate by picking an untested vice-presidential candidate in the mold of then-Alaska governor Sarah Palin, who became an outspoken heroine to conservatives but whom even many Republicans later acknowledged was unready to be a heartbeat from the presidency. As a result,

TABLE 2
Voters on the Economy

	Percentage who voted for Obama	Percentage who voted for Romney
Which ONE of these four is the biggest economic problem facing people like you?		
The housing market (8%)	63%	32%
Unemployment (38%)	54%	44%
Taxes (14%)	32%	66%
Rising prices (37%)	49%	49%
Should income tax rates:		
Increase for all (13%)	52%	44%
Increase only on income over $250,000 (47%)	70%	29%
Not increase for anyone (33%)	23%	75%
Who would better handle the economy?		
Obama (52%)	98%	1%
Romney (44%)	4%	94%
Is the U.S. economy:		
Getting better (39%)	88%	9%
Getting worse (30%)	9%	90%
Staying about the same (29%)	40%	57%
Do you think the U.S. economic system generally:		
Favors the wealthy (55%)	71%	26%
Is fair to most Americans (39%)	22%	77%

Source: ABC News 2012 Exit Polls, abcnews.go.com/politics/elections/National?ep=pre_na.

considerable speculation revolved around Ohio senator Rob Portman, a former U.S. trade representative and Office of Management and Budget director in the Bush White House, and former Minnesota governor Tim Pawlenty, who cochaired Romney's campaign after his own short-lived presidential bid. The thinking was that Romney would opt for competence over charisma.

But Romney came to believe that one Republican—Wisconsin's Ryan—offered him both qualities in abundance. As chairman of the House Budget Committee, Ryan had become an intellectual leader of his party by being the front man for the Republican push to reduce federal spending. His written manifestos, "A Roadmap for America's Future" and the subsequent "Path to Prosperity," made clear Ryan's view that Obama's decision to pass an economic stimulus law and make other expensive spending decisions without corresponding budget cuts were extremely ill advised. "This domineering government," he said of Obama's administration, "brings taxes, rules, and mandates; generates excessive levels of spending, deficits, and debt; leads to economic stagnation and declining standards of living; and fosters a culture in which self-reliance is a vice and dependency a virtue—and as a result, the entire country weakens from within."[14]

Ryan called for drastic reductions in spending and an overhaul of entitlement programs such as Medicare. That approach was worrisome to some Republicans; Gingrich famously dismissed it as "radical and right-wing social engineering" before repudiating those sentiments, and Obama himself had publicly disdained what he said was the congressman's insistence on balancing the budget on the backs of the poor.

Democrats questioned Ryan's credentials as a fiscal hawk, noting that his budget did not come into balance for several decades and that he dissented from the Simpson-Bowles deficit reduction commission's recommendations as a member of that bipartisan panel in 2011. (Ryan said his refusal to endorse the budget was based on his belief that it did not adequately address soaring health care costs.) But Ryan's efforts earned him wide respect from his House GOP colleagues, many of whom had made reining in spending a central focus of their election efforts.

At age forty-two, Ryan was a member of the "Young Guns" group of House Republican leaders along with Majority Leader Eric Cantor of Virginia and Majority Whip Kevin McCarthy of California, and possessed a confident speaking style. His articulation of conservative views made him a darling of conservative media outlets, bloggers, and pundits, and many of them had beseeched Ryan to enter the presidential race.

SAUL LOEB/AFP/GettyImages.

When Mitt Romney announced Wisconsin representative Paul Ryan as his vice-presidential running mate during a campaign rally after touring the USS *Wisconsin* in Norfolk, Virginia, in August, the move delighted conservatives—but Ryan ultimately could not even deliver his home state.

As a result, Ryan's selection as the vice-presidential nominee in August was seen as the best way for Romney to shore up his credentials with his party's right wing. Aides to Ryan said later that before he accepted Romney's offer, he had extensive conversations about his position as vice president, receiving assurances that he would play a central role on fiscal and economic matters, as Vice President Dick Cheney did on national security during George W. Bush's presidency.

The Medicare Debate

The selection of Ryan did firmly align Romney with what had become conservative mainstream thought—balancing budgets by slashing spending on social programs while cutting taxes to stimulate economic growth. But it also inaugurated a debate about Medicare that initially overshadowed the Republican desire to make the election a referendum on Obama's handling of the economy.

Democrats had made claims for years that their rivals intended to overhaul the health care program for the elderly, sometimes with great political success; Democrat Kathy Hochul won a 2011 special election for a House seat in a heavily Republican district in upstate New York by making that argument the centerpiece of her campaign.

The Romney-Ryan plan would institute a new premium-support plan beginning with new Medicare beneficiaries in 2023. Seniors would pick from private plans, or could choose traditional Medicare, all of which would be offered on a new Medicare exchange. Seniors could purchase private plans with government subsidies. The two men contended that some changes had to be made to Medicare because the system was going broke with the aging of the Baby Boom generation. Competition, Ryan argued repeatedly, would drive down costs. But Democrats portrayed those efforts as intended to dismantle the social safety net by giving people vouchers instead of a government guarantee of benefits. "We are for Medicare; they are for voucher care," Biden said in a theme he echoed repeatedly on the campaign trail.[15]

The Romney-Ryan campaign responded by frequently making the charge that Obama "robbed Medicare" to pay for his health care law. But independent sites such as FactCheck.org and PolitiFact noted that, although the health care law was slated to reduce the amount of future spending growth in Medicare, it does not actually cut Medicare—savings come from reducing money that goes to private insurers who provide Medicare Advantage programs, among other things. The Obama campaign also pointed out repeatedly that Ryan's own past budget blueprint had relied on the same $700 billion in savings from Medicare.

Obama was perceived as having the upper hand in the debate. A Gallup poll in September found that he had a 6-percentage-point edge, 50 percent to 44 percent, over who voters in twelve swing states trusted more on the issue.[16]

The Republican Convention: Overcoming the Empty Chair

Romney entered the Republican National Convention in Tampa, Florida, needing a jolt. He had made a highly publicized trip to several European countries that had been intended to bolster his stature on the international stage, but the news coverage was dominated by his criticism of England's management of the London Olympic Games and several other perceived "gaffes."' He had only recently begun airing biographical television advertisements that could help him establish a connection with voters, and he came to Tampa as the least-popular presidential nominee since 1988, according to the Pew Research Center.

Convention planners kept the focus squarely on Obama. Their theme for the first day was "We Can Do Better," a criticism of the president's tenure. Another was "We Built This," a jab at Obama's suggestion that entrepreneurs were not wholly responsible for their success. Romney's often-divisive primary opponents Perry, Cain, and iconoclastic libertarian representative Ron Paul of Texas were denied speaking roles at the convention. Instead, the party showcased several of its highest-profile minority members. They included Florida's freshman senator Marco Rubio, who won widespread praise—while touching off instant speculation about his 2016 intentions—for his story of being the son of immigrants who worked hard so that he could succeed.

In his speech, Romney expressed his empathy for the economically struggling: "[W]hen you lost that job that paid $22.50 an hour with benefits, you took two jobs at nine bucks an hour and fewer benefits." He gave his version of how Bain Capital had played a helpful role in the economy in starting companies such as office-supply giant Staples. But he kept the emphasis on Obama, citing what he called his rival's overly ambitious efforts to deal with climate change: "President Obama promised to begin to slow the rise of the oceans and heal the planet. My promise is to help you and your family."

Many observers found his address inadequate to the challenge. The influential D.C. publication *Politico* faulted him for not thinking big enough: "It is Romney, not Obama, who needs to somehow change the dynamic in some major way, and it is hard to see how Thursday's speech did this." Such a task was especially difficult because Romney was asking voters—in often fiery rhetoric—to abandon someone with whom they had made an emotional connection in 2008. Abandoning that connection "takes finesse and delicacy, Republican strategists say," wrote the *New York Times*'s Jim Rutenberg. "The sort of visceral attacks that conservative talk show hosts are calling for risk sending them into a defense posture on behalf of Mr. Obama and, more to the point, of their own decisions four years ago."[17] Perhaps as a result, Romney did not leave Tampa with the traditional post-convention upward "bounce" in opinion polls.

Ryan's convention speech, meanwhile, contained what the media characterized as a number of questionable claims. Even a contributor to Republican-leaning Fox News summed it up as "an apparent attempt to set the world record for the greatest number of blatant lies and misrepresentations slipped into a single political speech."[18] The Wisconsin congressman mentioned a shuttered GM auto plant in his hometown that he said Obama had promised to keep open; the plant had closed in December 2008 before the president took office. Such statements developed into a media narrative that Ryan only helped feed when it was later found that he had exaggerated his time in completing a marathon race.

AP Photo/Lynne Sladky, File.

Actor Clint Eastwood's rambling dialogue with an empty chair while speaking to delegates at the Republican National Convention in Tampa, Florida, will probably be remembered as one of the Romney campaign's biggest strategic gaffes.

But what made the Republican convention especially memorable was Clint Eastwood's appearance shortly before Romney on the final night. The acting and directing icon gave an unrehearsed, rambling presentation in which he directed many of his remarks to an empty chair onstage meant to represent Obama. Although the audience at the convention enjoyed the speech, and campaign officials later contended Romney did as well, there was no question that the address consumed precious political oxygen that Republicans had hoped would be allocated to more substantive subjects.

The Democratic Convention: A Helping Hand from Bill Clinton

At the Democratic convention in Charlotte, North Carolina, party officials showcased a much less ambitious theme than the uplifting messages of change that had propelled Obama into office. It boiled down to this: Thanks in large measure to the preceding decade's worth of problems he had inherited from George W. Bush—two wars, a crisis on Wall Street, and a severe housing-market downturn—the president's task of leading the country to an economic recovery was not yet finished. A Romney presidency, Democrats said, would only mark a return to the failed policies that caused those problems.

The central figure in making that case for Obama became former president Bill Clinton. The two men had never been close and at times were highly critical of each other, especially when Obama battled Hillary Rodham Clinton for the Democratic nomination. But Clinton had shaken off the melodrama of his affair with a White House staffer—and subsequent impeachment for lying under oath—and become a respected figure in his post-presidential years. A July 2012 Gallup poll found that two-thirds of Americans viewed him favorably, tying his record-high favorability rating at the time of his 1993 inauguration.[19]

As the convention's keynote speaker, the former president gave a detailed critique of Romney's plans while making the case that his successor's philosophy was firmly in line with his own—one that had delivered economic growth. Among other things, he said, the GOP sought to cut Medicaid spending by one-third over the coming decade. "Of course, that's going to really hurt a lot of poor kids," he said. "But that's not all. A lot of folks don't know it, but nearly two-thirds of Medicaid is spent on nursing home care for Medicare seniors who are eligible for Medicaid. It's going to end Medicare as we know it. And a lot of that money is also spent to help people with disabilities, including a lot of middle-class families whose kids have Down's syndrome or autism or other severe conditions."[20]

Even Republicans were impressed with how well Clinton crystallized the Democratic arguments. "This," GOP political consultant Alex Castellanos said on CNN after the speech, "will be the moment that probably reelected Barack Obama."[21]

Clinton's address—and the Democratic convention as a whole—was noteworthy in how it showcased the Affordable Care Act, a law about which a majority of Americans remained suspicious. The health care overhaul figured prominently in a video tribute to the late Massachusetts senator Edward M. Kennedy and was the subject of an entire speech by itself from Health and Human Services Secretary Kathleen Sebelius. "Obamacare is a badge of honor," she declared.[22]

In his own convention speech, Obama tried to present himself as humbled by the difficulty of reversing the economy but energized by the challenges ahead. He laid out his accomplishments and said they offered proof that he could deliver progress in the future. "The times have changed," he declared, "and so have I." His remarks received mostly middling reviews. Many observers said they sounded too much like his standard stump speech, with few big ideas. But they said the convention as a whole had been far better at making an argument for his party than the Republicans' effort to do the same.

September: A Tough Month for Romney

Obama received a boost in polls that continued even after the latest monthly unemployment survey—released the day after the Democratic convention ended—showed continuing sluggish job growth. Within weeks the poll "bounce" had faded, but he maintained a slim lead over Romney.

Corbis.

Former president Bill Clinton's speech at the Democratic National Convention praising President Obama was widely regarded—even by conservatives—as a political masterpiece for its folksy articulation of why Romney was the wrong choice.

The poll numbers were just one of several setbacks with which Romney had to contend in September. His campaign was forced to issue a series of clarifications about whether he would ban insurance companies from denying coverage for people with a preexisting medical condition. He said in an appearance on NBC's *Meet the Press* that he would retain the part of Obama's health care law that instituted the ban, but his campaign later qualified his statement to say Romney's proposal would apply only to those who already had coverage.

Meanwhile, Democrats, as well as some Republicans, upbraided him for his use of a foreign policy crisis in Libya that left four Americans dead to initiate a broader debate with Obama. The core of Romney's criticism was that the U.S. Embassy in Egypt sought to appease menacing protesters threatening their compound and did not immediately denounce them or Libyan protesters after U.S. diplomatic territory in both nations was compromised. But questions arose about whether Romney was too hasty in using the incident to blast his opponent amid a gathering threat. A lengthy article in *Politico* detailed what it said was considerable internal infighting among top aides.[23]

The biggest political harm to Romney came from the liberal magazine *Mother Jones*'s release of a secretly recorded videotape at a Florida fundraising event earlier in the year. In the video, Romney was heard saying: "There are 47 percent of the people who will vote for the president no matter what. All right, here are 47 percent who are with him, who are dependent upon government, who believe that they are victims, who believe the government has a responsibility to care for them, who believe that they are entitled to health care, to food, to housing, to you-name-it."

To Democrats, the comments cemented their depiction of him as unwilling to understand average Americans. Obama's lead jumped further in polls, and a *National Journal* anonymous survey of political insiders found that more than three-quarters of Republicans considered his remarks damaging.[24] Initially, Romney acknowledged that his comments were not artful, but said he was discussing politics, not policy, and that he stood by them. Several weeks later, however, he told Fox News that they were "completely wrong"—a shift that was widely characterized as part of his effort to maneuver back to the political center.

The Debates: Romney's Comeback

Romney and his advisers maintained that they were unfazed by losing ground, saying that the presidential debates would enable them to recover. And to be sure, the debates ended up taking on a greater role compared to those in other elections. At the first debate in Denver, which covered economic and domestic policy, the Republican was widely deemed to have scored a knockout against Obama, briefly changing the tenor of the race. Romney appeared in command and more comfortable than the president, who appeared passive and, to the surprise of many Democrats, chose not to bring up the "47 percent" remarks.

The two sparred in a series of exchanges over whether Romney had planned a $5 trillion tax cut (Obama said four times that he did, citing an independent analysis, but Romney emphatically denied it by saying it didn't take into account new revenue); whether Romney would reduce the share of taxes paid by the wealthy (something Obama said was at the heart of his rival's plan); and whether Romney would cut education funding (he said he had no plans to do so, despite his earlier vow to cut all nondiscretionary defense spending by 5 percent). To demonstrate he was a different politician than the one captured in the fundraising video, Romney said: "We're a nation that believes that we're all children of the same God, and we care for those that have difficulties, those that are elderly and have problems and challenges, those that are disabled."[25]

Despite what Democrats said were a number of factual errors on Romney's part, and despite his taking a variety of centrist positions at odds with his more conservative stands, Republicans were jubilant at his performance, and post-debate polls swung toward him (although there were no signs of a significant shift toward him in swing states). Obama did receive some comfort a few days later, when the

EPA/RICK WILKING/POOL Corbis.

At the first presidential debate in Denver in October, Romney was so forceful—and Obama so passive—that it caused considerable consternation among Democrats.

September unemployment rate dropped below 8 percent to register at 7.8 percent, the lowest level since he had assumed office. The development deprived Romney of what had been one of his key talking points.

Romney, however, was ready to broaden his message. He began turning up the heat on Obama's foreign policy record. Although polls found the president enjoyed a wide advantage over his challenger on that issue, Republicans continued to believe that the Middle East situation afforded them an opening. They continued to focus on the incident in the Libyan embassy, raising questions about the level of diplomatic security and citing the Obama administration's conflicting statements about when it knew the attack was the work of al-Qaeda-affiliated terrorists and not simply a random act.

In an October 8 address at Virginia Military Institute, Romney accused Obama of "passive" leadership in the region, saying: "Hope is not a strategy." Romney proposed more direct U.S. intervention in the ongoing conflict in Syria, including ensuring that anti-government opposition forces had weapons.[26] Romney also repeated his call for increased defense spending, but some of his critics lamented his unwillingness to spell out how it should be financed. Former secretary of state Colin Powell, who in October reendorsed Obama for president, summarized Romney's position as, "'Let's cut taxes and compensate for that with other things.' But that compensation does not cover all of the cuts intended or the new expenses associated with defense."[27]

FIGURE 3
Polling Averages for the General Election: Obama vs. Romney

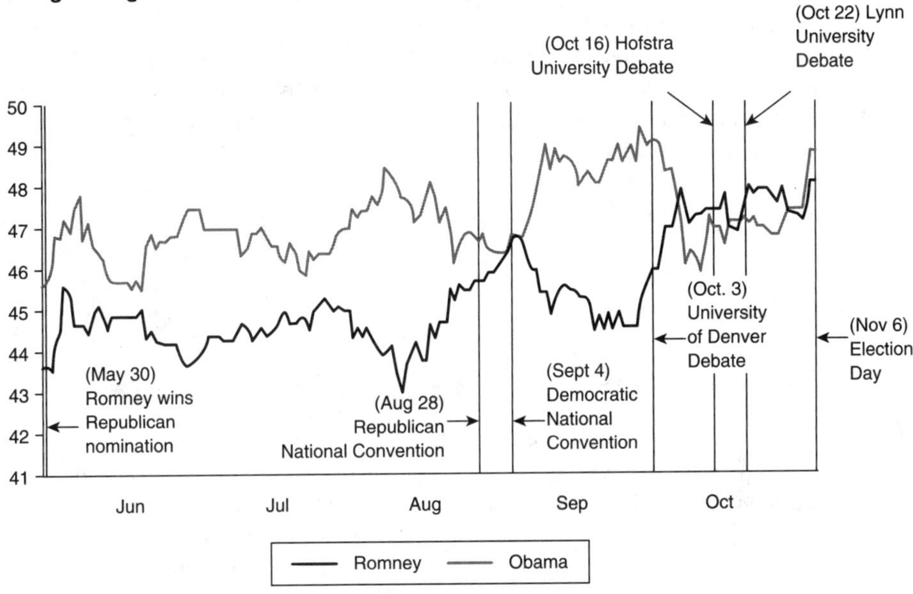

Source: Real Clear Politics, "General Election: Romney vs. Obama," www.realclearpolitics.com/epolls/2012/president/us/general_election_romney_vs_obama-1171.html, accessed November 14, 2012.

Ryan and Biden tackled foreign policy as well as other subjects in their lone vice-presidential debate three days later. Unlike Obama, Biden constantly challenged his rival, often grinning or laughing in disbelief as Ryan spoke. Ryan won praise for keeping his cool, though fact-checkers later pointed out that several of his claims—including one that "six studies" vindicated the mathematical plausibility of his ticket's tax plan—were, as Biden asserted, untrue (only two were academic; the others came from conservative think tanks). The conventional wisdom emerged that while both men did well, the vice president's feistiness and histrionics had reinvigorated a Democratic Party that was severely dismayed by Obama's earlier effort.

In the second encounter between Obama and Romney, a far more aggressive president showed up. He challenged Romney on his budget proposal, saying that his rival didn't have a five-point plan, as he often boasted, but a one-point plan—wanting the wealthy "to play by a different set of rules." The two men sparred at length about whether Obama had previously characterized the Libya attack as a terrorist incident until the moderator, CNN's Candy Crowley, told Romney that Obama had indeed done so. At the debate's end, Romney repeated his desire to care about "100 percent of the American people," which led to Obama's bringing up the "47 percent" comment. "Think about who he was talking about," Obama said. "Folks on Social Security who've worked all their lives. Veterans who've sacrificed for this country . . . . And I want to fight for them."[28] Most analysts concluded afterward that Obama convincingly won the debate, and his slide in the polls was arrested.

The final debate was devoted to foreign policy, though both candidates brought up domestic issues at length. Romney took a decidedly centrist tone that contrasted sharply with earlier campaign comments. Appearing determined to dispel any notions of him as a warmonger, he declared at one point about the Middle East: "We can't kill ourselves out of this mess." He even spoke positively about the United Nations, an organization reviled by many conservatives. On Syria, Romney tried to make the case that he would address the "tragedy" there without "having our military involved." But after Romney described working closely with allies in the region and helping to develop a coherent armed opposition, a visibly exasperated Obama retorted: "He doesn't have different ideas because we're doing what we should be doing."[29] Most analysts believed that the president won the debate, because Romney did not articulate why Obama needed to be replaced.

The Final Weeks: Making Their Closing Arguments

As the campaign entered the final weeks, both Romney and Obama began making serious plays for the handful of crucial swing states: Colorado, Ohio, Iowa, Florida, Virginia, Nevada, North Carolina, New Hampshire, Pennsylvania, Wisconsin, and Michigan. Even though Obama had lost ground in the national head-to-head polls to Romney, he had maintained a slim lead in swing-state polls, giving him an advantage in the Electoral College. *New York Times* polling analyst Nate Silver put Obama's chances at reelection above 70 percent, prompting widespread ridicule from conservative pundits.

To make his case, Romney gave an economic speech in Iowa in which he declared himself to be the candidate who could solve the "big problems" that Obama had promised he would tackle. Meanwhile, Ryan was regularly dispatched to his home state to implore Wisconsinites. Obama, for his part, made frequent forays from the White House into Virginia, where he jokingly dubbed as "Romnesia" his opponent's decision to soften his earlier conservative stands.

But the biggest prize remained Ohio. Polls showed Obama had maintained a small but persistent lead in the state, something attributed to the auto industry bailout. Romney aggressively sought to cut into that advantage, implying in a speech and subsequent TV ad that Chrysler was planning to move U.S. auto jobs to China. His claim was based on a news story that said Fiat, Chrysler's majority owner, planned to return Jeep output to the Asian nation. But the story also said that any Chinese production sites would be new ones making cars for Chinese buyers. Chrysler executives publicly rebuked Romney, and news media outlets characterized his stance as thoroughly deceptive. The flap led the Obama campaign to run ads questioning whether the Republican could be trusted on anything.[30]

As the campaign entered its final week, Romney trailed in Ohio but appeared to have momentum elsewhere. Such talk abated, however, when Hurricane Sandy bore down on the East Coast, causing widespread flooding and other damage in parts of New York, New Jersey, and other parts of the East Coast. The hurricane put both campaigns on hold for several days and gave Obama the opportunity to demonstrate

AP Photo/Pablo Martinez Monsivais.

Days before the election, President Obama embraces Donna Vanzant, right, during a tour of a neighborhood affected by Superstorm Sandy in Brigantine, New Jersey. The president's handling of the disaster not only won praise from Americans, but it effectively put Mitt Romney's campaign on hold during the crucial final days.

the power of the presidency. He traveled to New Jersey and met with GOP governor Chris Christie, who praised his efforts effusively.

Polls showed substantial numbers of voters—including 73 percent of likely voters in Ohio—approved of Obama's performance during the disaster, and senior Republicans lamented later that it deprived their candidate of the chance to talk about economic issues to sway last-minute undecided voters.

House, Senate, and Governors' Races

Key Senate Races

Republicans entered the 2012 election at a significant statistical advantage in the battle for Senate control. Whereas Democrats had to defend twenty-three seats,

Republicans had to defend just ten. Several Senate Democrats turned down the job of chairing the Democratic Senatorial Campaign Committee, the party's recruiting and fundraising arm, before Washington senator Patty Murray agreed to take the post. She had held the DSCC post in 2002, and though she doubled the committee's fundraising, she could not prevent her party from turning the Senate over to Republicans in that election.

Murray's Republican counterpart as chair of the National Republican Senatorial Committee was Texas senator John Cornyn, who also had held the job in the 2010 cycle. Cornyn was an ambitious conservative but more of a pragmatist than some of his colleagues. In several states where he believed hard-core conservatives stood less of a chance of winning, he recruited centrist candidates whose views offended the insurgent tea party element within the Republican Party. Cornyn was unapologetic, saying Republicans needed to broaden their appeal among independent-leaning voters.

In the end, however, Cornyn was unable to find enough candidates to suit his purposes. Democrats won twenty-two of the twenty-three races up for grabs; only Nebraska, where former senator Bob Kerrey lost to Republican Deb Fischer, was beyond their grasp. The twenty-two holds were the most by either party in a Senate election since 1964, when Democrats retained twenty-five of the twenty-six seats they were defending during President Lyndon Johnson's landslide reelection.

TABLE 3
The Senate

113th Congress		**112th Congress**	
Democrats	53	Democrats	51
Republicans	45	Republicans	47
Independents	2	Independents	2

Democrats	
Freshman elected	8
Incumbents reelected	15
Incumbents defeated	0
Republicans	
Freshman elected	3
Incumbents reelected	5
Incumbents defeated	1
Independents	
Freshman elected	1
Incumbents reelected	1
Incumbents defeated	0

Source: "Democrats Overcome Odds, Dominate Senate Elections," *CQ Weekly*, Election 2012 Special Report, November 12, 2012, p. 2228.

TABLE 4
2012 U.S. Senate Election Results

Candidate	Votes	Percent
Arizona		
Jeff Flake (R)	**875,794**	**50.0**
Richard Carmona (D)	797,019	45.5
California		
Dianne Feinstein (D)	**5,672,491**	**59.1**
Elizabeth Emken (R)	3,596,924	38.6
Connecticut		
Christopher S. Murphy (D)	**729,592**	**55.3**
Linda McMahon (R)	566,878	43.0
Florida		
Bill Nelson (D)	**4,479,315**	**55.2**
Connie Mack (R)	3,433,831	42.3
Hawaii		
Mazie K. Hirono (D)	**266,580**	**62.6**
Linda Lingle (R)	159,071	37.4
Indiana		
Joe Donnelly (D)	**999,840**	**50.1**
Richard E. Mourdock (R)	881,863	44.2
Maine		
Angus King (I)	**301,796**	**53.8**
Charlie Summers (R)	170,907	30.5
Maryland		
Benjamin L. Cardin (D)	**1,332,380**	**55.2**
Daniel John Bongino (R)	642,192	26.6
Massachusetts		
Elizabeth Warren (D)	**1,603,045**	**53.9**
Scott P. Brown (R)	1,372,068	46.1
Michigan		
Debbie Stabenow (D)	**2,566,547**	**58.2**
Peter Hoekstra (R)	1,698,264	38.5
Minnesota		
Amy Klobuchar (D)	**1,843,695**	**65.3**
Kurt Bills (R)	862,423	30.5
Mississippi		
Roger Wicker (R)	**660,174**	**55.6**
Albert N. Gore Jr. (D)	465,705	40.4
Missouri		
Claire McCaskill (D)	**1,484,683**	**54.7**
Todd Akin (R)	1,063,698	39.2

(Continued)

(Continued)

Candidate	Votes	Percent
Montana		
Jon Tester (D)	**200,265**	**48.3**
Denny Rehberg (R)	187,170	45.2
Nebraska		
Deb Fischer (R)	**445,443**	**58.2**
Bob Kerrey (D)	320,229	41.8
Nevada		
Dean Heller (R)	**456,640**	**45.9**
Shelley Berkley (D)	444,513	44.7
New Jersey		
Robert Menendez (D)	**1,785,499**	**58.4**
Joseph M. Kyrillos (R)	1,221,012	39.9
New Mexico		
Martin Heinrich (D)	**388,591**	**50.9**
Heather A. Wilson (R)	346,506	45.4
New York		
Kirsten Gillibrand (D)	**4,153,247**	**72.0**
Wendy Long (R)	1,530,713	26.5
North Dakota		
Heidi Heitkamp (D)	**160,752**	**50.2**
Rick Berg (R)	157,758	49.3
Ohio		
Sherrod Brown (D)	**2,621,380**	**50.3**
Josh Mandel (R)	2,351,136	45.1
Pennsylvania		
Bob Casey (D)	**2,899,659**	**53.6**
Tom Smith (R)	2,417,029	44.7
Rhode Island		
Sheldon Whitehouse (D)	**253,663**	**64.9**
B. Barrett Hinckley (R)	136,297	34.9
Tennessee		
Bob Corker (R)	**1,501,621**	**64.9**
Mark E. Clayton (D)	703,444	30.4
Texas		
Ted Cruz (R)	**4,443,133**	**56.6**
Paul Sadler (D)	3,174,617	40.5
Utah		
Orrin G. Hatch (R)	**589,217**	**65.1**
Scott N. Howell (D)	273,774	30.3
Vermont		
Bernard Sanders (I)	**197,461**	**71.2**
John MacGovern (R)	68,839	24.8

Candidate	Votes	Percent
Virginia		
Tim Kaine (D)	**1,905,853**	**52.3**
George Allen (R)	1,732,986	47.5
Washington		
Maria Cantwell (D)	**1,438,934**	**59.8**
Michael Baumgartner (R)	967,500	40.2
West Virginia		
Joe Manchin III (D)	**269,570**	**60.1**
John Raese (R)	164,895	36.8
Wisconsin		
Tammy Baldwin (D)	**1,528,143**	**51.5**
Tommy G. Thompson (R)	1,363,317	45.9
Wyoming		
John Barrasso (R)	**184,523**	**75.9**
Tim Chestnut (D)	52,595	21.6

D = Democrat
R = Republican
I = Independent

Source: "For the Record: Presidential, Gubernatorial, Senate and House Results," *CQ Weekly,* Election 2012 Special Report, November 12, 2012, pp. 2284–2293.

The Senate's final composition stood at fifty-three Democrats, forty-five Republicans, and two independents: Bernie Sanders of Vermont, who organized with the Democrats and voted with most of that party, and newly elected Angus King of Maine, who announced he would also caucus with the Democrats.

Democratic-Held States

Wisconsin. Rep. Tammy Baldwin became the Senate's first openly gay member, fighting past Tommy Thompson for the open seat of retiring Democratic senator Herb Kohl. Baldwin's sexuality was not an issue in the race, but it was an unrelentingly bitter contest. One outside analysis of both campaigns' advertisements found that over a thirty-day period, 99 percent were negative.

Baldwin was one of the House's most liberal members, and many observers questioned whether she could win beyond her base in the university town of Madison. But she ran a disciplined campaign, seeking to convince voters that she would be more attuned to the needs of Wisconsin than Thompson, a former governor who hadn't been a candidate for office in fourteen years. She downplayed her progressive views in favor of taking populist stands against China's trade policies and highlighting her work across the aisle. Her Democratic allies relentlessly portrayed Thompson as a Washington insider making money through his political connections.

The moderate Thompson's attempts to appear more conservative—he told a tea party group that he wanted to "do away with the Medicare and Medicaid," a departure from his previous positions—rang hollow with voters.

North Dakota. National Democrats also questioned whether they could successfully defend retiring senator Kent Conrad's seat in increasingly Republican-dominated North Dakota. But in beating GOP representative Rick Berg, Heidi Heitkamp played up her record as a straight-talking former state attorney general while running a centrist race that emphasized her policy disagreements with President Obama.

Heitkamp—who in 1986 succeeded Conrad as North Dakota's tax commissioner—stressed her independent views on issues such as energy, including her support for the controversial Keystone XL pipeline, and on spending. Heitkamp drew substantial attention for an advertisement in which she supported Obama's Affordable Care Act, which is unpopular in the state. She said the health care law

AP Photo/Andy Manis, File.

Some Democrats initially questioned whether Wisconsin's Tammy Baldwin could successfully run statewide, but she played down her liberal stands and talked more frequently about bipartisanship—a formula that other future candidates are likely to emulate.

contained "good and bad" and "needs to be fixed," but rebuked her opponent for voting to repeal it entirely.

In a state with such a small number of voters, Heitkamp relied heavily on being more affable than Berg, and was considered to have such a wide advantage in that area that one of Berg's key supporters publicly admonished voters not to simply pick the "most likeable" candidate.

Virginia. Having done Democrats a favor by chairing the Democratic National Committee, former governor Tim Kaine accomplished another in beating Republican George Allen for the seat held by retiring Democrat James Webb.

Kaine got into the Senate race at the urging of Democrats who were eager to find a high-profile challenger to Allen, also a former governor. Allen had previously held a Senate seat from 2001 to 2007 and his name was frequently mentioned as a potential presidential candidate. But Allen surprisingly lost reelection in 2006 to Webb, having sparked controversy when he referred to an Indian American aide to Webb at one of his rallies as a "macaca," an obscure term for monkey.

With their extensive political connections, both Kaine and Allen were able to flood the airwaves with ads. Allen also benefited from the outside group Crossroads GPS, which spent millions attacking Kaine. Allen ridiculed Kaine for accepting a position to head the DNC while he was still governor. For his part, Kaine hit Allen for past support of partial privatization of Social Security. Allen said he did not support changes for current retirees, but was open to a voluntary retirement investment plan as a supplement. Kaine also attacked Allen for increasing spending as governor.

Missouri. First-term senator Claire McCaskill initially was considered far and away to be the most endangered incumbent. Missouri has been becoming increasingly more Republican, and McCaskill's support for initiatives such as health care reform hurt her, as did some more personal issues such as failing to pay several years of personal property taxes on a jet owned by her husband.

But McCaskill was blessed by a drawn-out three-way Republican primary, and she got her wish when Rep. Todd Akin won the nomination. Akin was the most conservative of the primary candidates, calling Obama "a complete menace to our civilization," and McCaskill wasted no time in depicting him as an extremist who was out of step with most voters.

Akin's fate was sealed in August, when during an interview, he asserted that a woman's body could shut down and avoid pregnancy in cases of "legitimate rape." The comment prompted a political firestorm; Republicans from Romney on down called for him to drop out of the race. Though he refused to do so, his campaign never recovered.

Montana. Montana was another Republican-trending state in which first-term incumbent senator Jon Tester was seen as having an uphill chance. But Tester, known for his flattop haircut and regular-guy image, successfully persuaded voters that he hadn't "gone Washington" and beat Republican representative Denny Rehberg.

Tester cast himself as a moderate who wanted to break the partisan gridlock in Congress while emphasizing Rehberg's votes to cut off funding to Planned Parenthood and women's health clinics. He also took a page from the national Democratic playbook in sowing doubt about Rehberg's support for Social Security and Medicare. Although Rehberg got help from outside Republican groups, national Democratic interests from labor and women's groups came in to assist Tester, organizing a get-out-the-vote effort that proved effective.

Connecticut. Rep. Chris Murphy held off wealthy Republican Linda McMahon for the open seat of retiring incumbent Joe Lieberman, a Democrat-turned-independent. Murphy overcame attacks from McMahon about his poor attendance at congressional hearings as well as his failure to make timely rent and mortgage payments years ago.

Murphy criticized McMahon on issues affecting seniors, arguing that she would pose a threat to Social Security and Medicare. He also charged that her plan to cut taxes for the wealthiest earners wouldn't stimulate the economy. McMahon's personal finances were called into question after reports surfaced that she had been late on several property-tax bills.

But by tapping into her considerable personal wealth, McMahon spent exorbitantly on her campaign, burning through more than $42 million. She held moderate positions on some social issues and reversed course on a key gay-rights issue, saying that she would repeal the Defense of Marriage Act that defines marriage as the union of a man and a woman. Some, however, questioned her true ideological leanings, and the state's pro-Obama tilt ended up boosting Murphy.

New Mexico. Democratic representative Martin Heinrich won retiring five-term senator Jeff Bingaman's seat over former Republican representative Heather Wilson by portraying himself as a younger version of Bingaman: a deliberate thinker interested in science and devoted to protecting the federal government's large New Mexico presence. Like Bingaman, he advocated expanding energy production through a broad range of sources.

A former Air Force officer and National Security Council staffer, Wilson was the political protégé of popular former GOP senator Pete Domenici and was considered one of her party's most formidable 2012 candidates. In running against Heinrich, she stressed her independence from her party, but Democrats painted her as too conservative. Heinrich accused her of withholding her plan to address entitlement programs' financial shortfalls while cutting spending. Wilson consistently trailed Heinrich in polls, eventually prompting national Republicans to turn their attention elsewhere.

Ohio. Liberal Democratic senator Sherrod Brown had been regarded as vulnerable, particularly in a presidential year in which Republicans devoted so much energy to Ohio. But Brown and other Democrats were able to define his opponent, thirty-five-year-old Republican state treasurer Josh Mandel, as overly ambitious and not ready for the responsibilities of the Senate.

The U.S. Chamber of Commerce, Crossroads GPS, and other outside Republican-backed groups spent nearly $20 million in Ohio to defeat Brown—more than any other single race—by criticizing his support for Obama's stimulus and health care overhaul. But like Obama, Brown successfully tapped into the state's blue-collar populist sentiment; his campaign went so far as to publicly threaten to tow any imported non-U.S.-made cars that were parked at its headquarters.

Republican-Held States

Massachusetts. Democrats accomplished one of their biggest goals of the 2012 election by successfully helping Harvard law professor Elizabeth Warren topple Sen. Scott Brown, who had won a 2010 special election for the seat that had been held for decades by Sen. Edward M. Kennedy.

Warren chaired the Congressional Oversight Panel for the $700 billion Troubled Asset Relief Program, and in 2010 and 2011—as an assistant to Obama and special adviser to Treasury Secretary Timothy Geithner—she helped design and launch the Consumer Financial Protection Bureau, a legacy of the Dodd-Frank legislation aimed at reforming Wall Street. Her work earned Warren the enmity of the financial industry, and Republicans blocked her expected appointment as the bureau's first director.

Yoon S. Byun/*The Boston Globe* via Getty Images.

Harvard professor Elizabeth Warren's victory raised hopes among liberals that she could become one of their champions of the Senate, but to accomplish much legislatively, Warren realized she would have to emphasize collegiality and avoid letting her fame get in the way.

But Warren became a national sensation when a speech she gave, exhorting wealthy Americans to recognize the debt they owe to the community and "pay forward for the next kid who comes along," went online. Money poured into her campaign, and Warren held her own in debates with Brown, who repeatedly rebuked Warren for claiming that she had Cherokee ancestry. It was a ruse, Brown's supporters said, that Warren used to exploit affirmative-action plans. Warren denied it, and won the election with ease.

Indiana. Next to Missouri representative Todd Akin's comment about "legitimate rape," the election's most incendiary remark came from Republican Senate candidate Richard Mourdock, who suggested that pregnancies resulting from rape are "something that God intended to happen." But in the GOP-leaning state, there were other reasons that Democratic representative Joe Donnelly appealed to independent voters: a moderate voting record and unflashy style that helped reassure Hoosiers that he could be a viable successor to iconic six-term Republican senator Richard Lugar, also a moderate.

When Mourdock, the Indiana state treasurer and a favorite of the tea party, ousted Lugar in the GOP primary, his supporters saw the general election largely as a formality. But within hours of winning the nomination, Mourdock made several appearances on television shows suggesting that he didn't believe in compromise. That allowed Donnelly and Democrats to paint him as an extremist, a view that their rival's later comment only exacerbated.

Maine. In a state that prides itself on its political independence, Maine's popular former governor King ran an entirely nonpartisan campaign—he would not say which party he would caucus with if elected—and established himself as the early front-runner. He never relinquished that status to his major-party rivals and was elected to succeed retiring moderate Republican senator Olympia Snowe.

National Democrats recognized King's unique stature and did little to support their nominee, state senator Cynthia Dill. To help the Republican nominee, Maine secretary of state Charlie Summers, the conservative nonprofit Crossroads GPS ran ads blasting King's support of tax hikes as governor. The National Republican Senatorial Committee also broadcast an ad accusing King of using political connections to win a "sketchy" federal loan guarantee to build an industrial wind farm. But such attacks gained little traction against such a known political commodity.

Nevada. Republican representative Dean Heller was appointed in April 2011 to fill the unexpired Senate term vacated by scandal-plagued Sen. John Ensign. Democrats immediately marked him as one of their top targets, but Democratic representative Shelley Berkley could not capitalize on Obama's success in Nevada and Senate majority leader Harry Reid's robust get-out-the-vote operation that had won his reelection two years earlier.

Democrats attacked Heller for his voting record on Medicare and Social Security, for his support of the Ryan budget plan, and for the contributions he had taken from business. Republicans, in turn, portrayed Berkley as a rubber-stamp for Democrats' legislative agenda, and focused on the fact that she was under investigation by the House Ethics Committee on charges that she used her position for personal financial gain.

Arizona. In a surprisingly competitive race, Democrat Richard Carmona came close to knocking off Republican representative Jeff Flake for the seat vacated by retiring GOP senator Jon Kyl, but Arizona's GOP orientation helped give Flake the victory.

Carmona ran on the strength of his resume as a decorated Army combat veteran and former U.S. surgeon general, vowing to be an independent who would work with both parties. He attacked Flake on a number of issues, including a charge that he would open the Grand Canyon to mining and that he has voted against the interests of veterans. Flake responded to the criticism of his record on veterans with a powerful television ad accusing Carmona of having anger issues. Flake also highlighted his long-standing opposition to earmarks.

Texas. Republican Cuban-American Ted Cruz's successful bid to succeed retiring GOP senator Kay Bailey Hutchison—which came after he easily dispatched a primary opponent who had the strong backing of Texas's Republican establishment—was seen as an affirmation of the tea party movement's power. His victory prompted immediate comparisons to Florida senator Marco Rubio, another young conservative Latino on the rise.

AP Photo/David J. Phillip.

Along with Florida senator Marco Rubio, newly elected Texas senator Ted Cruz immediately was seen by Republicans as someone who potentially could lead alienated Hispanic voters back to the party.

Cruz was expected to be no match for Lt. Gov. David Dewhurst, who had not only millions of dollars to throw into the race but also the backing of almost every prominent state Republican, including Texas governor Rick Perry. Cruz sank $1 million of his own money into the contest shortly before the primary and held Dewhurst to under 50 percent of the vote to force a runoff. From there, Cruz attracted the backing of conservative heavyweights such as former Alaska governor Sarah Palin and former senator Rick Santorum of Pennsylvania, as well as outside groups such as the Club for Growth and Freedom Works. Cruz ultimately trounced Dewhurst by fourteen percentage points. From there, he had little trouble beating his Democratic opponent in the general election, former Texas House member Paul Sadler.

Utah. Republican senator Orrin Hatch successfully eluded the tea party's determination to duplicate its success in ousting Republican senator Robert Bennett in 2010 for being insufficiently committed to its agenda. Once known for his ability to work with Democrats to cut deals, something that incensed tea party members, Hatch became a staunchly uncompromising and outspoken voice on the far right. Though he could not avoid a runoff after Utah's Republican state party convention, Hatch easily dispatched former state senator Dan Liljenquist, 66 percent to 34 percent. In heavily Republican Utah, that put him in position to win a seventh term by easily defeating former state Senate minority leader Scott Howell in the general election.

Key House Races

Few observers gave Democrats much of a chance to reclaim the majority that they had won back in 2006 and then lost in 2010. Redistricting followed its traditional pattern of shuffling around various groups of voters for the sake of protecting certain incumbents—Republicans, in most states—and ended up making too many House seats unwinnable for the opposition. The Democrats ended up picking up fewer than half the twenty-five seats they had needed to reassume control, thus ensuring that the House would remain a powerful check on Obama's second-term plans.

The power of redistricting in the GOP's favor was underscored by a *Washington Post* analysis: According to the ballots counted as of Nov. 9, Democrats actually won more of the House vote nationwide—roughly 48.8 percent compared to 48.47 percent for Republicans.[31]

Romney's failed presidential bid ensured that House Speaker John Boehner, R-Ohio, would remain his party's most powerful elected official. The fact that he would have to continue to work with Obama for at least two more years increased the speculation that the speaker would have to be far more flexible in making deals than he previously had been. In a post-election conference call with his caucus, Boehner emphatically drove home that point.

But it would be no easy task for the Ohioan. Most of the largely conservative eighty-seven-member Republican class of 2010 won reelection, and their ranks were bolstered by another three dozen Republicans elected in 2012, most of them just as conservative as their predecessors. Neither Boehner nor his top lieutenants—Majority

TABLE 5
The House (as of November 30, 2012)

113th Congress		**112th Congress**	
Republicans	234	Republicans	240
Democrats	200	Democrats	190
Pending runoffs	1	Vacancies	5

Republicans	
Freshmen elected	35
Incumbents reelected	199
Incumbents defeated	16
Democrats	
Freshmen elected	44
Incumbents reelected	152
Incumbents defeated	10

Note: Louisiana Republican Reps. Charles Boustany and Jeff Landry were scheduled to face each other in a December 8, 2012 runoff election.

Sources: "Redistricting a Winner for GOP and Democrats," *CQ Weekly*, Election 2012 Special Report, November 12, 2012, p. 2247, and "Election 2012: Results," CNN.com, http://www.cnn.com/election/2012/results/main

Leader Eric Cantor of Virginia and Majority Whip Kevin McCarthy of California—could deliver their home states for Romney, something that the conservative members of his party were keen to note. "So, we're not impressed so much with their political strategy," one freshman member told *National Journal*.[32]

California. The nation's largest state also saw more turnover in the House than did its counterparts. An independent redistricting commission redrew California's political map, while new rules required the top two finishers in a primary to face each other in the general election even if they represented the same party.

The result was that several veteran House members were unable to retain their seats. Among them was forty-year incumbent Democrat Pete Stark, who lost his race representing a portion of San Francisco's Bay Area to Democrat Eric Swalwell, a Dublin city councilman. Democratic representative Brad Sherman beat a fellow incumbent member of his party, thirty-year veteran representative Howard Berman, in an acrimonious contest to represent Los Angeles's San Fernando Valley.

Minority Democrats made substantial gains in the Golden State. State senator Gloria Negrete McLeod ousted San Bernardino–area Democratic representative Joe Baca after getting a last-minute infusion of money from New York City mayor Michael Bloomberg, who strongly opposed Baca's pro-gun-rights stance. And Democrat Raúl Ruiz fulfilled one of his party's long-held aspirations in knocking off Republican representative Mary Bono Mack to represent the Palm Springs region. Meanwhile, Japanese American Mark Takano picked up an open seat in the Riverside area to become the first openly gay person of color to hold a seat in Congress.

Florida. In an election that featured plenty of nasty battles, some of the nastiest took place in the Sunshine State. Freshman Republican representative David Rivera sought reelection to his Miami-area seat amid accusations of political wrongdoing during the primary campaign and a criminal investigation into a separate matter, only to lose to Democrat Joe Garcia.

To the north, GOP representative Allen West—a favorite of the tea party known for his blunt attacks on Democrats—lost to Democratic challenger Patrick Murphy, who overcame West's attempt to use his 2003 arrest in a bar brawl against him. Democrats also returned to office Alan Grayson to represent a redrawn Orlando-area district. Before losing in 2010, Grayson had distinguished himself as one of his party's most vocal critics of Republicans.

Illinois. After losing four House seats in 2010, Democrats in President Obama's adopted home state dethroned three GOP incumbents representing parts of the Chicago area and a fourth representing the state's western prairie. Veteran representative Judy Biggert and freshmen representatives Joe Walsh, Bobby Schilling, and Robert Dold all became victims of Democratic-engineered redistricting—the party controlled the governorship and both houses of the state legislature—that made it much tougher for their party.

AP Photo/Pablo Martinez Monsivais.

Democrat Patrick Murphy of Florida won over GOP representative Allen West, a favorite of the Tea Party. Although polls showed Murphy was the clear winner, West refused to immediately concede in the hotly divisive race.

Overall, five of the state's six new House members were Democrats. The battle for the state's two competitive open seats was a draw, as each party managed to keep the one they controlled.

New York. As in Illinois, Democrats demonstrated their dominance. Democrat Dan Maffei reclaimed the Syracuse-area seat he lost two years earlier to Republican Ann Marie Buerkle, while former Clinton White House staffer Sean Patrick Maloney unseated Nan Hayworth, another Republican elected in 2010, to represent New York City's northern suburbs.

The Republicans' lone bright spot in the state was Chris Collins's ability to topple Democratic representative Kathy Hochul for the seat representing Buffalo's socially conservative, working-class suburbs.

North Carolina. The Tarheel State was one of just a handful of states in which Republicans were able to win back Democratic-held House seats. Republican former congressional staffer Richard Hudson turned back Democratic representative Larry Kissell in Charlotte's suburbs, while Republican activist Mark Meadows took back a seat for his party in western North Carolina. In addition, GOP former prosecutor George Holding won a divisive primary that enabled him to coast to a general-election win for the Raleigh-area seat of retiring Democratic representative Brad Miller. Democratic Representative Mike McIntyre withstood a tough challenge from Republican challenger David Rouzer.

Governors' Races

Along with the White House and Congress, Republicans made a priority of gaining governorships. The Republican Governors Association raised about twice as much money as its Democratic counterpart, and the GOP ended up with chief executives in thirty statehouses—the biggest number held by either party in twelve years.

But the election still registered as a disappointment to the party. Only one state—North Carolina—switched from Democrat to Republican, as former GOP Charlotte mayor Pat McCrory defeated Democratic lieutenant governor Walter Dalton to become that state's first GOP governor since 1993. McCrory narrowly lost his first gubernatorial bid in 2008 to Democrat Bev Perdue, who faced sagging public approval ratings and decided against reelection.

In some of the states that resisted GOP takeovers, the strong Democratic tide helped candidates of that party. But in others, voters decided that the pressing issues that led many of them to back Republicans at the federal level did not extend further downward.

Washington. The state anchoring the Pacific Northwest emerged in recent years as one of the nation's most consistently Democratic voting. The last Republican to win for president was Ronald Reagan in his 1984 landslide, Democrats hold both Senate seats, and the party had a seven-election winning streak for governor entering 2012. But some of those governor's races have been nail-biters, no more so than the 2004 contest in which Christine Gregoire defeated Republican Dino Rossi by 133 votes, or

TABLE 6
2012 U.S. Gubernatorial Election Results

Candidate	Votes	Percent
Delaware		
Jack Markell (D)	**275,547**	**69.3**
Jeffrey E. Cragg (R)	113,792	28.6
Indiana		
Mike Pence (R)	**994,437**	**49.5**
John R. Gregg (D)	936,592	46.6
Missouri		
Jay Nixon (D)	**1,485,961**	**53.9**
David Spence (R)	1,157,475	42.6
Montana		
Steve Bullock (D)	**201,236**	**48.8**
Rick Hill (R)	196,199	47.5
New Hampshire		
Maggie Hassan (D)	**336,339**	**54.4**
Ovide M. Lamontagne (R)	263,543	42.7
North Carolina		
Pat McCrory (R)	**2,421,926**	**54.7**
Walter H. Dalton (D)	1,912,966	43.2
North Dakota		
Jack Dalrymple (R)	**199,769**	**63.1**
Ryan M. Taylor (D)	108,622	34.3
Utah		
Gary R. Herbert (R)	**617,784**	**68.3**
Peter Cooke (D)	251,555	27.8
Vermont		
Peter Shumlin (D)	**161,081**	**58.0**
Randy Brock (R)	104,893	37.8
Washington		
Jay Inslee (D)	**1,232,847**	**51.1**
Rob McKenna (R)	1,177,791	48.9
West Virginia		
Earl Ray Tomblin (D)	**225,949**	**50.0**
Bill Maloney (R)	207,612	46.0

less than one-hundredth of a percentage point. Gregoire won a more comfortable six-point margin in a 2008 rematch with Rossi, but her decision to retire created an open-seat race.

Both parties settled early on their nominees, with Democrats choosing eight-term U.S. representative Jay Inslee and Republicans tapping state attorney general Rob

McKenna. Inslee ran on a platform of protecting education funding and targeting tax breaks and aid toward clusters of industries, such as clean energy and life sciences, to eke out a narrow victory over McKenna.

New Hampshire. Democratic former state senator Maggie Hassan and Republican attorney Ovide Lamontagne waged a competitive race to replace retiring Democratic governor John Lynch. Lamontagne was the better known of the two candidates as a result of his chairmanship of the state Board of Education and earlier unsuccessful bids for governor and the U.S. Senate. But Hassan campaigned on a promise to govern in much the same manner as the popular Lynch, which proved to make the difference.

Missouri. In a state that has become increasingly Republican, Democrat Jay Nixon won a second term over Republican businessman Dave Spence. Nixon won praise from fiscally conservative voters for cutting expenses rather than raising taxes and for working with GOP lawmakers to develop and implement a five-year strategic plan focused on job retention and creation. He also was commended for his management during several natural disasters.

West Virginia. Democrat Earl Ray Tomblin became governor in November 2010 when then-governor Joe Manchin resigned to assume his new duties as the state's junior U.S. senator. A special election to fill the remainder of Manchin's term was held in October 2011, and Tomblin won the race over Republican businessman Bill Maloney. Thirteen months later, Tomblin won a full term by again beating Maloney. He steered clear of national politics and, like Manchin, made abundantly clear his dissatisfaction with Obama, a deeply unpopular figure in the state.

Indiana. Republican Mike Pence, a high-profile member of the U.S. House GOP leadership, won by amassing a sizeable edge in campaign spending over Democratic former state House Speaker John Gregg. Also giving Pence a boost was the popularity of outgoing Republican governor Mitch Daniels, who at one point was a serious candidate for president before deciding to forego the race.

Lessons Learned from the 2012 Elections

Perhaps above all else, the 2012 elections showed just how hardened the partisan lines have become on both ends of the political spectrum. It proved demographers' earlier observations that the United States has become a self-segregating nation, with voters increasingly choosing to live around like-minded people.

This divide between "Red America" and "Blue America" has grown as the nation has developed its own separate information networks—through the Internet and news media—that increasingly have encouraged the demonization of the other side, making bipartisanship extremely difficult.

In the thirty-two states that supported Democrat Bill Clinton for president in 1992, forty-four Democrats and twenty Republicans held those states' seats in the Senate—a sign that Republicans could win even in Democratic presidential states. But the twenty-six states that voted for Obama in 2012 sent forty-three Democrats and just nine Republicans to the Senate. Only five Senate candidates won election in states that the other party's presidential nominee won—and the number would have been lower if not for the self-destructive campaigns of Republicans Richard Mourdock in Indiana and Todd Akin in Missouri.

In House races, Democratic victories over incumbent Republicans occurred mainly in the Northeast, West, and upper Midwest. Republicans, meanwhile, won Democratic seats almost exclusively in the South, in states such as Arkansas, Kentucky, North Carolina, and Oklahoma. The one Democratic governorship that the GOP picked up was in North Carolina, another southern state; over the past decade, the party has gained control over nineteen of the twenty-four legislative chambers in the South.

All of this meant that despite President Obama's convincing reelection victory, he continued to lead an extremely divided nation through a fragile coalition made up of minorities and white urbanites, as well as white working-class voters in a few Midwestern states. Many of its key demographics—especially younger voters—do not participate as much in off-year elections, which could add to the Democratic Party's troubles in the 2014 midterm elections.

To unite the disparate elements of his party, Obama proposed dealing seriously with immigration reform, with a few Republicans—most prominently Sen. Rand Paul, a hero of the tea party movement—agreeing to work with him. The president also made clear that his victory gave him political clout on many of the economic issues on which he campaigned, such as increasing taxes on the wealthy.

But it remained to be seen whether he could make another prominent issue—climate change—a major focus of his second term. In the immediate aftermath of the election, Democrats were more interested in smaller, easier-to-pass measures such as increasing energy efficiency. The sweeping cap-and-trade bill that Democrats steered through the House in 2009—but that sank in the Senate in the face of unanimous Republican opposition that it would harm businesses—appeared extremely unlikely to be resurrected.

Along those same lines, it was hard to imagine that Obama's endorsement in 2012 of same-sex marriage—a cause that advocates described as nothing less than the civil rights issue of the 2000s—would gain much traction. He said he preferred to leave the matter up to the states and that it was something probably best left to future generations.

In all, it was apparent that the issues that led Obama's supporters to reelect him were not ones most dear to the Republican Party, such as balancing budgets through sharply reduced spending. As a result, the partisan gridlock that led so many to condemn Washington so bitterly was not likely to go away anytime soon.

Endnotes

1. "President Obama's Acceptance Speech," *Washington Post,* www.washingtonpost.com/politics/decision2012/president-obamas-acceptance-speech-full-transcript/2012/11/07/ae133e44-28a5-11e2-96b6-8e6a7524553f_story_3.html, November 7, 2012.

2. Ronald Brownstein, "The American Electorate Has Changed, and There's No Turning Back," *National Journal,* November 8, 2012.

3. Beth Reinhard, "Color Scheme," *National Journal,* November 8, 2012.

4. Richard Viguerie, "The Battle to Take Over the GOP Begins Today," www.conservativehq.com/node/10743, November 7, 2012.

5. Steve Holland, "Romney Clinches 2012 GOP Nomination in Texas," Reuters, May 30, 2012, mobile.reuters.com/article/topNews/idUSBRE84T02720120530?i=2.

6. Michael Gerson, "A GOP That's Off Track," *Washington Post,* November 7, 2012.

7. Michael R. Bloomberg, "A Vote for a President to Lead on Climate Change," Bloomberg.com, www.bloomberg.com/news/2012-11-01/a-vote-for-a-president-to-lead-on-climate-change.html, November 1, 2012.

8. Jim Rutenberg and Jeff Zeleny, "Romney Camp Seeks to Head Off Post-Convention Anxieties," *New York Times,* September 10, 2012.

9. Rodney Hawkins, "Biden: Romney Won't Disclose Tax Loopholes He'll Close," *National Journal,* September 9, 2012.

10. Steve Shepard, "Poll: Romney Supporters More Engaged, But Not Because of Him," *National Journal,* June 21, 2012.

11. Yochi Dreazen, "Democrats Renew Attacks on Romney's Money," *National Journal,* August 2, 2012.

12. "Mitt Romney Says Barack Obama Began His Presidency With an 'Apology Tour,'" PolitiFact, www.politifact.com/truth-o-meter/statements/2012/oct/17/mitt-romney/mitt-romney-says-barack-obama-began/, October 17, 2012.

13. Major Garrett, "The Confidence Game," *National Journal,* September 1, 2012.

14. U.S. House Budget Committee, "The Roadmap Plan," roadmap.republicans.budget.house.gov/plan/#Intro.

15. David Jackson, "Biden: GOP Would Turn Medicare Into 'Voucher Care,'" *USA Today,* September 3, 2012.

16. Andrew Dugan, "Swing-State Voters Trust Obama More to Address Medicare," Gallup.com, www.gallup.com/poll/157613/swing-state-voters-trust-obama-address-medicare.aspx, September 24, 2012.

17. Elspeth Reeve, "What They're Saying About Mitt Romney's Big Speech," AtlanticWire.com, www.theatlanticwire.com/politics/2012/08/what-theyre-saying-about-mitt-romneys-big-speech/56408/, August 31, 2012.

18. Sally Kohn, "Paul Ryan's Speech in Three Words," Fox News.com, www.foxnews.com/opinion/2012/08/30/paul-ryans-speech-in-three-words/, August 30, 2012.

19. Lydia Saad, "In U.S., Bill Clinton at His Most Popular," Gallup.com, www.gallup.com/poll/156362/bill-clinton-popular.aspx, July 30, 2012.

20. "Bill Clinton's Speech at the Democratic National Convention," *Washington Post,* www.washingtonpost.com/politics/dnc-2012-bill-clintons-speech-at-the-democratic-national-convention-excerpt/2012/09/05/f208865e-f7a4-11e1-8253-3f495ae70650_story.html, September 5, 2012.

21. Kevin Cirilli, "Pundits Swoon Over Bill Clinton's Speech," *Politico*, September 5, 2012.

22. Jill Lawrence, "Five Most Surprising Things About the Democratic Convention," *National Journal*, September 7, 2012.

23. Mike Allen and Jim VandeHei, "Inside the Campaign: How Mitt Romney Stumbled," *Politico*, September 16, 2012.

24. Naureen Khan and Peter Bell, "Insiders: 47 Percent Comment Damaging," *National Journal*, October 4, 2012.

25. "2012 Presidential Debate," WashingtonPost.com, www.washingtonpost.com/politics/decision2012/2012-presidential-debate-president-obama-and-mitt-romneys-remarks-in-denver-on-oct-3-running-transcript/2012/10/03/24d6eb6e-0d91-11e2-bd1a-b868e65d57eb_story.html, October 3, 2012.

26. Sarah Huisenga, "Romney Proposes New Sanctions on Iran, New Help for Syrian Rebels," *National Journal*, October 8, 2012.

27. "Colin Powell Endorses Barack Obama for President," CBS News.com, www.cbsnews.com/8301-505263_162-57539893/colin-powell-endorses-barack-obama-for-president/, October 25, 2012.

28. "Full Transcript of the Second Presidential Debate," *New York Times*, www.nytimes.com/2012/10/16/us/politics/transcript-of-the-second-presidential-debate-in-hempstead-ny.html?pagewanted=all&_r=0, October 16, 2012.

29. "Transcript of the Third Presidential Debate," *New York Times*, www.nytimes.com/2012/10/22/us/politics/transcript-of-the-third-presidential-debate-in-boca-raton-fla.html?pagewanted=all, October 22, 2012.

30. Jill Lawrence, "Romney Ad Wrongly Implies Chrysler Is Sending U.S. Jobs to China," *National Journal*, October 28, 2012.

31. Aaron Blake, "Democratic House Candidates Winning the Popular Vote Despite Big GOP Majority," *Washington Post*, November 9, 2012.

32. Billy House, "The Speaker's Moment," *National Journal*, November 8, 2012.